GETTING TO KNOW
THE U.S. PRESIDENTS

J O H N
A D A M S

SECOND PRESIDENT
1797 – 1801

WRITTEN AND ILLUSTRATED BY MIKE VENEZIA

CHILDREN'S PRESS®
A DIVISION OF SCHOLASTIC INC.
NEW YORK   TORONTO   LONDON   AUCKLAND   SYDNEY
MEXICO CITY   NEW DELHI   HONG KONG
DANBURY, CONNECTICUT

Reading Consultant: Nanci R. Vargus, Ed.D., Assistant Professor, School of Education, University of Indianapolis

Historical Consultant: Marc J. Selverstone, Ph.D., Assistant Professor, Miller Center of Public Affairs, University of Virginia

Photographs © 2004:
Archive Photos/Getty Images: 4, 5
Bridgeman Art Library International Ltd., London/New York: 26 (Delaware Art Museum, Wilmington, Howard Pyle Collection), 15, 20 left, 20 right (Massachusetts Historical Society, Boston, MA), 23 (Museum of Fine Arts, Boston, gift of Joseph W. Revere, William B. Revere, and H. R. Revere), 30 (New-York Historical Society, New York, USA), 16 (Private Collection)
Harvard University Art Museums: 32 (Harvard University Portrait Collection, Bequest of Ward Nicholas Boylston to Harvard College, 1828, image © 2003 President and Fellows of Harvard College, Photographic Services, John Adams (1735-1826), by John Singleton Copley, 1783, oil on canvas, 238 x 147 cm)
Library of Congress: 27
Museum of Fine Arts, Boston: 22 (Deposited by the City of Boston, Samuel Adams, about 1772, by John Singleton Copley, American, 1738-1815, oil on canvas, 49 1/2 x 39 1/2 in., L-R 30.76c)
North Wind Picture Archives: 19, 21
PictureHistory.com: 24
Superstock, Inc.: 3 (National Gallery of Art)
U.S. Department of the Interior, National Park Service, Adams National Historical Park: 10, 11

Colorist for illustrations: Dave Ludwig

Library of Congress Cataloging-in-Publication Data

Venezia, Mike.
   John Adams / written and illustrated by Mike Venezia.
      p. cm. — (Getting to know the U.S. presidents)
Summary: An introduction to the life of John Adams, an influential
patriot during the American Revolution who became the nation's first
vice president and second president.
   ISBN 0-516-22607-X (lib. bdg.)   0-516-27476-7 (pbk.)
   1. Adams, John, 1735-1826—Juvenile literature. 2. Presidents—United
States—Biography—Juvenile literature. [1. Adams, John, 1735-1826. 2.
Presidents.] I. Title. II. Series: Getting to know the U.S. presidents.

E322.V46 2004
973.4'4'092—dc21

                                    2002156744

A portrait of John Adams by Gilbert Stuart (National Gallery of Art, Washington D.C.)

John Adams was the second president of the United States of America. He was born in Braintree, Massachusetts, in 1735. Because he was cranky a lot of the time and kind of arrogant, John Adams wasn't the most popular president.

Although John Adams was short-tempered and thought a lot of himself, he had many good qualities, too. His friends, the people he worked with, and even his enemies always respected his intelligence, generosity, honesty, and courage. Nothing could stop John Adams from fighting for freedom and American independence.

John Adams (standing at table, first on the left) was one of the signers of
the Declaration of Independence.

John Adams grew up on his parents'
farm in Braintree. His grandfather, great
grandfather, and great-great grandfather all
had been farmers.

John's parents always believed in the importance of education. They taught their son to read when he was very young.

John loved going to school at first, but
when he was about eight or nine years old, he
started going to a larger school. Things didn't
go well for John at his new school. He couldn't
stand it!

John said his teacher, Mr. Cleverly, was
the dullest and laziest man he ever knew.
Mr. Cleverly taught only Latin, and he didn't
do a very good job of it.

John Adams felt that Mr. Cleverly ruined his desire to go to school. In fact, John was so upset that he started to skip school altogether!

John spent his days making and sailing toy boats, flying kites, playing marbles, and hunting. John always enjoyed the countryside and rocky seaside near Braintree.

John Adams was born in this red farmhouse in Braintree, Massachusetts.

When Mr. Adams found out what was going on, he was quite upset. He wanted John to get good grades so that he would be able to go to college. John told his father he didn't want to go to college and that he wanted to be a farmer. To change John's mind, Mr. Adams took him out early the next morning and made him do some of the hardest farming jobs.

At the end of the day, Mr. Adams was surprised to find that his son still wanted to be a farmer. John actually enjoyed the hard work.

Finally, however, Mr. Adams convinced John how important a good education was. He agreed to send John to a new school. John liked his new school and teacher a lot. He began to enjoy studying and reading again.

John Adams did so well in school that he got into Harvard College at the age of sixteen. Harvard was near the city of Boston, Massachusetts. When John Adams graduated, he decided to become a lawyer.

Harvard College in the early 1700s

When John Adams began his career as a lawyer, Massachusetts was one of thirteen colonies in North America that belonged to Great Britain. Great Britain was the most powerful kingdom in the world. It was headed by George III, King of England. For many

years, people in the colonies got along pretty well with the British government. Suddenly, however, things started to go wrong.

King George III of England

The king of England needed more money for his country. He began forcing the colonists to pay extra fees for supplies that were shipped from England to the colonies. These extra fees were known as taxes.

John noticed that more and more people in the colonies were becoming annoyed. No one liked having to spend extra money on things they needed, such as sugar, tea, paint, lead, and silk cloth.

One tax law the colonists really hated was the Stamp Act. This act taxed almost every piece of paper in the colonies— newspapers, books, business documents, calendars, and even playing cards! These things all had to be stamped to show that the tax had been paid. The extra money went to the English king.

An example of the type of stamp forced on colonists by the Stamp Act

John Adams was especially upset with the Stamp Act. He was married now and had a hard enough time supporting his wife, Abigail, and their new baby daughter without paying extra taxes. John Adams began to write articles in the newspaper about how unfair the English government was being. Other colonists preferred to protest more violently, though.

Portraits of Abigail Adams and John Adams by Benjamin Blythe (Massachusetts Historical Society)

John Adams' friend Paul Revere created this illustration of the Boston Massacre.

On March 5, 1770, an angry mob attacked a group of British soldiers in Boston. The soldiers fired their guns into the crowd and some colonists were killed. The event became known as the Boston Massacre.

The soldiers who fired into the crowd were in big trouble. No one in the colonies wanted to defend them in court. No one, that is, except John Adams. John Adams felt that no matter how bad a crime seemed, those who were accused always deserved a fair trial.

John Adams took a big risk doing this. Some people called him a traitor. He angered many of his friends, including Paul Revere and Samuel Adams, John's cousin. But many people thought John Adams did something very important. He had the courage to do the right and fair thing.

A portrait of Paul Revere by John Singleton Copley (Museum of Fine Arts, Boston)

John Adams was becoming well known in Massachusetts and in the rest of the colonies. He was always being asked to run a committee or to take on some government job. John knew things were getting worse and worse between the colonies and England.

One night, angry colonists threw tons of English tea off boats into Boston Harbor.

An illustration showing the Boston Tea Party

They were tired of paying taxes on the tea. To teach the colonists a lesson, King George III closed the harbor. He sent thousands of soldiers to guard the area. He also demanded that the colonists feed the soldiers and give them a place to sleep.

A painting by Howard Pyle showing the Battle of Lexington

Finally, the colonists decided that they had had enough. Before long, battles between British soldiers and the colonists broke out in the towns of Lexington and Concord, Massachusetts.

The leaders of the colonies decided to break away from England and start a new nation. They made it official with a Declaration of Independence. John Adams was on the committee to help put the declaration together. John had also nominated George Washington to head America's new army. The Revolutionary War had begun.

John Adams was asked to travel to France and ask for its help in fighting the British. John spent almost ten years in Europe finding ways to aid his new American country. He eventually helped work out the peace agreement that ended the Revolutionary War.

This unfinished painting by Benjamin West shows John Adams (seated at left) gathered with others to sign the Treaty of Paris, which ended the Revolutionary War.

Soon after John Adams returned home to his brand-new country, George Washington was elected the nation's first president. John Adams was elected vice president. Eight years later, after Washington's second term ended, John Adams was elected second president of the United States of America.

When John Adams began his new job, he had all kinds of problems to solve. The most serious one was that France, which had once been a friend of the United States, started attacking American ships. They took cargo and arrested American sailors!

A United States ship battling a French ship in 1799

Some American warships began fighting back. Many people wanted to go to war with France, but John Adams thought that would be a big mistake. He had just started up the U.S. Navy, and knew it wasn't ready for a big war with a powerful nation like France.

It wasn't long before people started to criticize the way President Adams was handling the French problem. To try to stop people from complaining so much, the president and his supporters did something that turned out to be a bad idea. They came up with and passed some new laws. One, called the Sedition Act, said that anyone who criticized the government could be thrown in jail! To most people, the law seemed like something a king, not the president of the United States, might do.

A portait of John Adams by John Singleton Copley (Harvard Portrait Collection)

As president, John Adams often did things only the way *he* wanted. Usually, he wouldn't even listen to his friends' suggestions. Because of his stubbornness, John Adams wasn't popular enough to be voted in for a second term as president.

John Adams is probably best remembered for his courage and for his great ideas that helped make the thirteen colonies into the United States of America. John Adams died at the age of ninety-one on July 4, 1826—exactly fifty years after the approval of the Declaration of Independence.